MW00946934

THE **SEVEN PHASES** OF FINANCIAL WELLNESS

THE **SEVEN PHASES** OF **FINANCIAL WELLNESS**

A Simplified Personal Finance System That Will Transform How You View Money

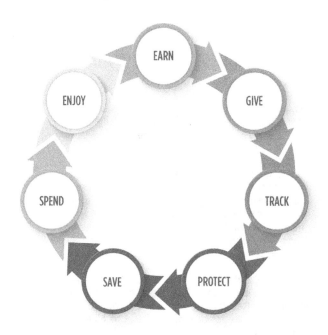

JOE BROWN

XULON PRESS

Xulon Press
2301 Lucien Way #415
Maitland, FL 32751
407.339.4217
www.xulonpress.com

© 2021 by Joe Brown

All rights reserved solely by the author. The author guarantees all contents are original and do not infringe upon the legal rights of any other person or work. No part of this book may be reproduced in any form without the permission of the author.

Due to the changing nature of the Internet, if there are any web addresses, links, or URLs included in this manuscript, these may have been altered and may no longer be accessible. The views and opinions shared in this book belong solely to the author and do not necessarily reflect those of the publisher. The publisher therefore disclaims responsibility for the views or opinions expressed within the work.

This book is for educational and informational purposes and should not be solely used in lieu of consulting legal, tax, and licensed financial professionals. Results may vary and are not guaranteed. Author assumes no liability for any injury, action or other items resulting from this book.

Unless otherwise indicated, Scripture quotations taken from the Holy Bible, New International Version (NIV). Copyright © 1973, 1978, 1984, 2011 by Biblica, Inc.™. Used by permission. All rights reserved.

Library of Congress Control Number: 2021906312

Paperback ISBN-13: 978-1-6628-1463-1
Hardcover ISBN-13: 978-1-6628-1464-8
Ebook ISBN-13: 978-1-6628-1465-5

TABLE OF CONTENTS

Introduction. vii

Why Phases? ix

Phase 1- EARN 1

Phase 2- GIVE 13

Phase 3- TRACK 21

Phase 4- PROTECT. 29

Phase 5- SAVE 43

Phase 6- SPEND. 53

Phase 7- ENJOY 67

Action Plans 75

INTRODUCTION

The person who instilled in me the importance of financial wellness was my father. He was born during the Great Depression. Many people of his time either put all their trust in the U.S. economy (through the stock market) or none of it. My dad was the latter and had little trust in financial institutions, but he was a saver and taught me how to save as well. I was that kid who went to the arcade with a $10 roll of quarters. In the seventies, that would last the entire day because the arcade games only cost a quarter. My dad also personified DIY. He could fix almost everything, and that allowed him to buy rental units and do all the repairs. His pension and rental income allowed him to retire in his forties and live the second half of his life without the constraints of a 9 to 5 job. He lived a very simple life and bought everything with cash, including his cars and even his real estate properties.

Nearly 100 years after the birth of my father, the world is bit more complicated, but good financial principles stand the test of time. When I became a father, I taught my children the value of money by teaching them how to save using the classic piggy bank or toy cash register. As they got older, I expanded to it to a system of giving, saving, and spending. For many years, I also taught my students to manage their finances in that order— give, save, and spend. There are too many financial systems available to count, but most are very complicated or need a financial professional to interpret them for you. Because financial matters are so complicated, most people either give all their trust to a professional or struggle along with no real success in their finances. There is a happy medium, and that is the system I developed after many years struggling and making mistakes that lead to things like home foreclosure, car repossession, and even bankruptcy. I have ignored the cultural norms and gone back to simple principles and actions that helped my dad live through the Great Depression and several world wars, developing a system called, "The Seven Phases of Financial Wellness." These are things that we should have been taught in grade school and high school but were not. Sadly, many colleges fail to teach these principles and practices as well. These seven things or phases can be used to guide and evaluate your personal finances regularly and consistently. The phases are in sequential order, but as in a project, many items happen at the same time. As you grow in each area, you will begin to see how they work together and will experience increased financial wellness day after day, week after week, month after month, and year after year.

WHY PHASES?

I have spent nearly thirty years of my life as a project manager. During that time, I have managed hundreds of projects ranging from thousands to millions of dollars in total budget. Whether large or small, every project required the ability to take complex systems and activities and translate them into easy-to-understand concepts for my clients. Any given project can have hundreds or thousands of action items, and they can get very confusing for the average person. Assigning the various tasks to a phase helped me as the project manager to convey the complexities of a project in a simple and straightforward manner to my clients. Each phase represents a major set of activities or action items. So, instead of saying we are on item number or step 325, I can say that we are in phase two of a seven-phase project. These phases are in sequential order, but sometimes there is overlapping of phases. At the same time, the phases are sequential because some items in a phase must happen before you can move to the next phase. For example, from a monthly budgetary basis, you should not spend before you save or save before you give or give before you earn. But you should always be tracking and protecting. You will see how they all work together as you progress through this book.

Like my many real estate and construction projects, personal finances can be very complex, and no one can be an expert in every area. There is an infinite number of things to know about investing, insurance, banking, etc., but I discovered there are seven basics things you do with money over and over throughout your life. These seven things or phases make up the system I developed, "The Seven Phases of Financial Wellness." The seven phases are: **Earn** money, **Give** money, **Track** money, **Protect** money, **Save** money, **Spend** money, and **Enjoy** money. You will be able to easily understand and regularly evaluate your personal finances in these areas and see how you grow in your financial wellness.

PHASE 1 - EARN

**A lazy person will end up poor,
but a hard worker will become rich.
Proverbs 10:4 (NCV)**

The Problem: Income for the average person is far below his or her earning potential. Lack of effort or an unwillingness to change how you make money will halt your progress. Too many people have a get- rich-quick mentality, when they should have a long-term view of wealth building.

The Solution: Learn to make wise financial decisions and apply the diligent habits of high income earners. Grow your income over time.

PHASE 1 - EARN

My first real job was a summer job I worked in my mid-teens at the local Naval shipyard. I then worked at a summer camp and finished high school working at a local fast-food restaurant. I liked the feeling of being independent and not having to depend on my parents or anyone else to afford my lifestyle. Since that first summer job, there has never been a long period in my life when I haven't had part-time or full-time income. After high school at the age of seventeen, I enlisted in the U.S. Army and spent the next few years there before enrolling in college. While in college, I continued to serve out my military obligation with the National Guard. One of the things that attracted me to my university was that they offered a co-op program. The program helped student find short-term employment while still enrolled in school, which provided valuable work experience in your chosen major and hopefully would lead to full-time employment after graduation. The program basically allowed students to take off a semester or two to work full-time and then return to school for one or two semesters during their sophomore and junior years. I worked both of my co-op assignments with the same company and even worked part-time while in school. I never had to look for a job after school because my company hired me with a big raise once I earned my degree. Although I have had many other sources of income, I have been able to work full-time with this company in project management for nearly thirty years.

I wish I could say that I have built a vast business empire over the last thirty years, but like many Americans, I have basically lived off my earned income. (I fully explain what earned income is later in this chapter) I am thankful that I was able to support my family while doing a job a really enjoyed. In addition, the retirement investing matching that my company offers has allowed me to grow a significant retirement savings.

The year 2020 was a difficult one for many individuals and businesses worldwide. Despite the difficulties of the 2020 pandemic, I believe my ability to follow the principles and practices I teach in the book allowed my family and I to get through the crisis without any major financial setbacks. In fact, my income and net worth grew. I have always practiced the philosophy, "Where there is a will, there is a way." I hope this chapter expands your knowledge of the many ways to earn, but more so, I hope it challenges your will to pursue your earning potential and never give up.

Do the Work

There's no substitute for hard work. I know people say that you must work smart and not hard, but hard work is smart. I would agree that you should think of more efficient ways of doing some jobs and that you should pursue income streams where you are not always trading time for money. There are only so many hours within a week, and your income can only grow exponentially when you learn to harness the work of others. So purpose to do hard work in a smart way with the belief that it will pay off.

Mindset

You will never do the hard work if you don't believe it will pay off. How you think about yourself will often determine your outcome before you even move a muscle. Many people practice positive affirmations to reprogram their sub-conscious mind. Many people or businesses have had great success because of their vision. They saw the desired outcome in their mind long before they realized it. You must believe in yourself, or you will defeat yourself long before you begin to exercise the actions that will produce your desired outcome.

In addition to believing in yourself, you must live a life of gratitude. There is always something in your life that is worth expressing gratitude for. Don't live your life always comparing yourself to others, but appreciate what you have now while you strive for greater heights. Don't try to live like a millionaire on a $100,000. The "Joneses" are not as happy and well off as you think. Live within your means and don't try to emulate a life that looks like a storybook until you look deeper and realize that everyone has problems and issues that they wish they didn't have in their lives.

Focus on Serving Others

Many of the most successful products/services became successful because they filled a void or need in the marketplace. If you serve enough people, the financial rewards are sure to follow.

Harness the Power of Questions

In order to get an answer, more often than not, you must ask the right question. If you ask the right questions, you will get the right answers. If you ask lousy questions, you will get lousy answers. If you ask great questions, you will get great answers! Questions create the challenges that make us learn. Continually ask yourself thought-provoking questions. Add to the questions at the end of each chapter and see your life transform for the better.

Common Characteristics of Successful People

- They are exceptional at what they do.

> When you work hard and aim to be the best, number one, leader of the pack, you distinguish yourself far above your competition to the extent that you really eliminate it. Many top businesses' revenue is more than double their closest competitors'.

- They are very hard to replace.

> When you eliminate your competition, you become hard to replace. Many businesses purchase "key man" insurance so their company does not suffer a catastrophic loss as the result of losing the most important member of their team.

- They are in high demand.

> When you eliminate your competition and become hard to replace, you consequently become in high demand. Would you want the second-best heart surgeon if you could afford the best heart surgeon?

Employees vs. Entrepreneurs

Generally speaking, employees have no financial interest in their company and are totally at the mercy of their employer. Where as, entrepreneurs have a financial interest in their company and have a say about how the business is run. Employees are not concerned about customer retention, but entrepreneurs are. Employees' salaries don't automatically increase based on company profits, but entrepreneurs income does increase based on company profits. Employees are not compensated based on their efforts, but on their job description. Entrepreneurs are compensated based on their efforts and the efforts of others. Even if you are a highly paid employee, find some way to engage in an entrepreneurial endeavor.

As an employee, you basically trade your time for money. You have a job. A self-employed person, basically owns a job. You have more say and more income potential, but if you don't work, you don't get paid. A business owner may have been someone self-employed who decided to hire someone who could do his or her job. Business owners now have the potential to a greater income because they can get paid by the efforts of others, even if they are not working. Business owners can develop their own system or buy into a pre-established system, like a franchise or network marketing business. Investors have the greatest income potential because they make money from the efforts of others with little to no day-to-day involvement with the company. They provide capital (money) to the business in exchange for a share of the profits.

In short, aim to be a "boss"—if not a boss in position, at least a boss in attitude. In other words, walk, talk, and act like a boss. Have an entrepreneurial spirit. To quote a friend of mine, "Be an entrepredoer." Carry yourself with swagger and confidence. Don't have an obnoxious attitude, but distinguish yourself as a person of value and importance like the successful characteristics discussed above. Financial freedom also gives you confidence and allows you to act like a boss. I would rather be someone debt-free making $50,000 per year and have $50,000 in savings then someone laden with debt making $100,000 a year with no savings. The former has options and less job pressure, while the latter may look rich but is stressed out and would likely end up homeless within a short time of losing his or her job. **Your income should not decrease your freedom but should increase it.**

Each of Us Is the Sum Total of Our Daily Habits or Routines.

The key or secret to succeeding in any endeavor in life is to learn from those who are doing/being what you'd like to do and/or be and duplicate their habits and actions. If an overweight man wants to lose weight, he should learn from someone who was once overweight and figured out how to lose weight and keep it off. If you want to be a great boxer, you should learn from other great boxers. Not only will you learn what to do, but you will learn what not to do. So, if you want to earn more, you should study those who are earning more. Even if you can't immediately duplicate their accomplishments, you can immediately duplicate their habits. Each of us is the sum total of our daily habits or routines.

A bit of advice: Try to make every day successful because daily habits turn into weekly habits, weekly to monthly, and soon, your lifestyle. Evaluate yourself periodically. For example: I made a goal to read the entire Bible in one year. It was broken into daily readings. By the end of the year, I had only read about 75 percent of the Bible. Although I didn't entirely reach my goal, I succeeded in reading 75 percent of what most people never read in a lifetime. Aim for the stars, but the view from the mountaintop isn't bad either.

A Chief Habit of the Rich

Most rich people have multiple streams of income.

Seven Common Kinds of Income Streams:

(Aim to get residual income, which pays you over and over based on one transaction.)

Earned Income: Working a Job. You can be a highly-paid executive or a cashier, but you still have a boss to answer to. Rarely is this residual because you are basically trading time for money.

Capital Gains Income: Income from assets that have increased value like real estate, vintage cars, art, etc.

Dividend Income: Income from stocks that is disbursed periodically, rather than reinvested for future capital gains.

Profit Income: buying and selling of goods and/or services. Buying low and selling high. The difference between the buy price and sell price is the profit.

Rental Income: having tenants that pay you monthly rental payments.

Royalty Income: monetizing your ideas to get paid for books, songs, trademarks, patents, etc.

Interest Income: lending money and charging a percentage fee, like banks, pawnshops, and mortgages.

Common Business Organizations:

SOLE PROPRIETORSHIP
A sole proprietorship has unlimited liability and single taxation.

LLC (Limited Liability Corporation)
An LLC has limited liability and single taxation.

C CORP
A C Corp has limited liability and double taxation.

Start or Join a Business to Accelerate Income Potential

If you are not a high-income earner and want to be more than an employee earner, you must start, join, or buy an existing business to boost your income. There are two major concerns to consider before starting a business, and they are: liability and taxes.

These two concerns overlap with items in other phases, like: Protection (Phase 4), Saving (Phase 5), and Spending (Phase 6). The right business structure, sometimes combined with insurance, can protect you from catastrophic loss.

The right business structure can also help you lower or avoid certain taxes, which will decrease your spending and increase your savings. In general, the tax laws benefit business owners more than they do wage earners or employees.

Consult with your attorney and/or tax professional to maximize your benefits in these two areas.

Success Stories. There's Hope for You.

Sam Walton started Walmart when he was forty-four years old and died the richest person in America. His heirs are still one of the richest families in the world.

Colonel Sanders didn't become a professional chef until he was forty years old, didn't franchise KFC (Kentucky Fried Chicken) until he was sixty-two years old, and wasn't a household name until he sold the company in his seventies.

Samuel L. Jackson was forty-three when he landed his first major role and now has been in more than 180 films.

We spend more time of our life working than any other activity. Make that activity count.

Pursue your full potential.

Live your dreams.

Q&A (Questions & Actions)

Are you happy with your current income?

What products or services does the world need?

What would you do if you could not fail, if there were no limitations in money, resources, time, or networks?

Who inspires you the most? Why?

If you only have one stream of income, aim to add another stream over the next few weeks. Check out the link below and consider the Business Builder option. For less than $100, you can start a business that has the potential to make you money while you sleep. https://jbrown1x3.wearelegalshield.com

Create a daily activity/routine that leads you closer to your dream job.

Create a poster that depicts your dream job. Use several pictures and quotes.

PHASE 2- GIVE

It is more blessed to give than to receive.
Acts 20:35b

Problem: Selfishness drains you, and few people benefit in the long run by being selfish.

Solution: Being generous strengthens you and sets you up to be blessed in every area of your life.

PHASE 2- GIVE

I have always been a generous person. It's not that I give money to every proverbial hand that is out, but I find it hard not to meet a need when I have the means to do so. The pastor of the first church I joined in my late teens recognized me for my willingness to give as a teenager. That particular church posted the giving amounts of the members for everyone to see. The giving records were not posted in a special room or discreet location but in the front lobby for members and visitors alike to freely view. I am sure there were mixed opinions about the need for the records to be displayed publicly, but I wasn't ashamed at someone seeing my giving amounts. I didn't give to get recognition, but I felt and realized that I was giving back a portion of something that had been given to me.

Just about twenty years ago, the "financial floor" collapsed beneath my family. My youngest daughter was sick and was in the hospital more than she was home. My wife had to take a leave of absence from her job to tend to her. The absence of her paralegal income started to become more apparent as the medical cost increased beyond what our insurance would cover and the mortgage company foreclosed on a second property we owned. The last thing that preceded us filing for bankruptcy was our leased minivan being repossessed. I did my very best to make good on the mounting charges; I contacted the credit card company for help, but they just quoted regulations at me. I offered to pay back the mortgage payments, but they wanted the entire borrowed amount; and I reclaimed my repossessed vehicle only to have it repossessed again. At the same time, I was enrolled in school (seminary), and the tuition bill was fast approaching. I had already filed for bankruptcy, and I committed to not incur any more deb. That decision, and a few acts of generosity, would turn my financial future around for good. Firstly, my school increased my grant so I could avoid going into debt to attend school, and then, the most surprising and unexpected gift was given to my wife and me. My neighbor witnessed the repossession of our vehicle and decided to bless us with a gift. We came to the door and saw an envelope addressed to us. Inside was a note that read, "God told us to give this to you," along with a check for $2,000. We were very grateful to them and to God for this, and we were determined not to let these gifts be given in vain. I want to recreate the tremendous feeling of joy I felt by giving to others and hope that the gifts encourage their hearts as much as our neighbor's gift did ours. Lastly, the gifts kept coming because my daughter was completely healed and is in her second year of college at a prestigious Ivy League university with no student loans.

I hope my story impresses to you the change a gift can have on your financial future and the future of those you give to. As your finances improve, you can then impact lives on a larger level, which will encourage you to make more so you can amplify the impact your giving has in your sphere of influence and the world.

Giving Actually Makes You Happy

There have been scientific studies done that actually show that giving activates chemicals/hormones in our brain that make us happier. They have been nicknamed the "be happy hormones." There has also been plenty of research that suggests that happy/ optimistic people have a lower risk of stroke, heart disease,

and other ailments, which leads to longer lives. Practice uncon-
ditional giving with "no strings attached," meaning, you trust
the receiving person or organization to responsibly use the gift
how they see fit.

Basic Ways to Give

There are many ways to give, but it basically comes down to
the three T's: (Time, Talent, & Treasure).

A person giving of his or her time could be someone who volunteers. Many organizations rely on volunteers to accomplish
the primary functions of their mission and could not operate
effectively without them. Mentoring a young man or young
woman could alter his or her course in life. Your generosity can
certainly come from sharing your schedule/time with others.

A person who gives of his or her talent can be someone with
a particular skill or gift that would otherwise be too expensive
for someone to afford to hire. This could be an architect who
builds houses for the poor, a doctor who provides free medical
care to underserved communities, or a lawyer who provides
legal services free of charge. There are always people who can
benefit from a service they cannot necessarily afford.

And finally, a person who gives of his or her treasure provides
needed financial resources to a cause. There are philanthro-
pists who dedicate a significant portion of their funds to various causes, but the smallest donation can go a long way when
coupled with other donations and managed wisely.

We all can find some way to give, whether big or small. If you
are a part of a faith-based organization, then I suggest you
start there with your giving. If not, there are still many causes
that you can dedicate a portion of your income to. Depending
on the amount you decide to donate, you could even consider
starting your own charitable organization. This world has been

enriched by the generous donations of kind people throughout history. Set aside an amount in your budget and begin to give very soon.

Imagine it's Christmastime, and you see the expression on a child's face when receiving his or her favorite toy/gift. If you could, would you freeze that moment in time to relive the joy that fills the room? Even though you cannot freeze the moment, you can recreate it by giving regularly. Giving allows us to express love more than receiving or taking ever will. There is even a holiday set aside to show our appreciation for what we have been given—we call it Thanksgiving. Giving even extends beyond your life by having a well-thought-out estate plan. I have never seen a hearse pulling a storage van. Giving is the action that counteracts greed. **Don't just be a receiver; be a giver.**

Q&A (Questions & Actions)

What's the top priority in your life right now?

Have you ever had someone give you an unusually special gift?

How did that make you feel?

Have you ever given someone an unusually special gift?

What was his or her reaction?

On your next payday, set aside a small amount to give away.

Over the next few weeks, find an organization that is doing something you can stand behind and begin to regularly and consistently give to that organization.

If you are already giving, consider increasing your gift.

PHASE 3- TRACK

**Be sure you know the condition of your flocks,
give careful attention to your herds;
Proverbs 27:23 (NIV)**

Problem: It is impossible to effectively organize and manage your finances without knowing what is coming in and going out.

Solution: You should have a budget/spending plan that accounts for every dollar coming in and every dollar going out. This cash flow plan should be adjusted monthly to account for your unique expenses that month.

PHASE 3- TRACK

Keeping records has never been a struggle for me, but it was not until I kept track of every dollar coming in and going out that my savings began to grow like never before. For years, I had kept a ledger detailing all the bills I paid. I began to notice that I had "more month than money." In other words, all my bills I recorded did not exceed my monthly income, but I found myself regularly going into my savings to finish the month. I had several checks bounce, and I could not figure out why. I initially though it was a bank error, but that wasn't it. I had been teaching finances and neglected an essential practice key to really tracking my finances. I was tracking the major expenses but ignoring the small, incidental ones. After reading several books and watching several videos, I once more became a serious student of finance and began to track every expense. After several months of budgeting every dollar coming in and going out, I soon realized that I was spending myself into poverty. My major budget buster was food. I was eating out for breakfast, lunch, and dinner. I was not spending high amounts, just five or six dollars here and there, but it actually added up to around $500 per month. I had discovered that the source of my monthly money shortage was my eating habits. I began using an app on my phone so I could list all my income and expenses and update it as I spent money. I made the necessary adjustments and eliminated bounced checks, grew my savings, paid off debt, and regained control of my finances all within a two-year timespan. I now have a fully funded emergency fund, no consumer debt (only a mortgage), and money left over every month. A budget is the primary tool that helped me get where I am today.

What Is a Budget?

MONTH (PLAN EACH MONTH/ NO YEARLY BUDGET)		
INCOME	PROJECTED (INITIAL)	PROJECTED (CORRECTED)
PRIMARY INCOME (TAKE HOME)	3000	3000
OVERTIME	200	500
PART-TIME	50	100
Other 1		
Other 2		
TOTAL (INCOME AND EXPENCES SHOULD MATCH)	3250	3600
EXPENCES	PROJECTED (INITIAL)	PROJECTED (CORRECTED)
GIVING (10%-15%)		
TITHES	50	300
OFFERINGS	10	10
OTHER	5	50
SAVING (10%-15%)		
EMERGENCY FUND	0	300
RETIREMENT (15%)	0	0
HOUSING (25%-35%)		
MORTGAGE/RENT	1000	1000
ELECTRIC	150	150
GAS	150	150
WATER AND SEWER	50	50
CABLE	200	0
PHONE		40
CELL PHONE	125	45
INTERNET	0	40
OTHER		
TRANSPORTATION		
CAR PAYMENT (LIST IN DEBT)		
BUS FARE	96	96
GASOLINE	60	0
CAR WASH		
MAINTINENCE		
OTHER		
FOOD		
GROCERIES	215	275
DINING OUT	185	50
OTHER		
LIFESTYLE		
CLOTHING	100	25
HAIR	120	60
DRY CLEANING	75	25
GYM MEMBERSHIP	35	10
DAYCARE	600	325
TUITION		
PETS		
GIFT		
OTHER	50	50
OTHER		
INSURANCE		
HOME/RENTERS		
AUTO	200	0
LIFE		
HEALTH		
DISABILITY		
LONG-TERM CARE		
OTHER		
DEBT		
CAR NOTE	400	0
STUDENT LOAN	105	105
DEPARTMENT STORE	75	75
PERSONAL LOAN	65	65
CREDIT CARD	33	33
CREDIT CARD	26	271
OTHER		
OTHER		
TOTAL	4180	3600
DIFFERENCE	-930	0

A budget is a tool you use to effectively manage or track your expenses and the resources that God has blessed you with. A budget is like putting a GPS tracker on every dollar. It is not restrictive but actually frees you up to give, save, and spend without worry or regret.

Budgeting Tools

Old fashioned pencil and paper	Software programs
Ledger tablets	Internet-based programs
Computer spreadsheets	Smart phone apps (my top tool of choice)

Prioritize Your Budgeting

How you structure your budget is very important. After you list all your sources of income, I suggest you list and pay your most important expenses first. (see budget chart) The necessities like rent/mortgage, transportation, and food should proceed items like a cable bill, subscriptions, and debt payments. Car payments should rise in priority if car is used to get you to work. The goal should be to eventually eliminate all debt. If you train yourself to pay the most important expenses first, then months when your income does not exceed your expected expenses, you will handle the major items prior to handling the minor items. Remember to give first, save second, and spend last.

Keep all your financial documents well-organized and in a secure place. For emergencies, your spouse or someone else close to you should know the location of these important documents.

Partial List of Documents

Leases/mortgage deeds	Birth/death/marriage certificates
Passports	
Vehicle titles	Military records
Insurance papers	Wills/trust documents
Important contracts	

In addition to creating a budget and organizing your important documents in one place (ideally a fire proof safe), complete a net worth statement that provides a snapshot of your overall financial standing.

NET WORTH STATEMENT

CATEGORY	SAMPLE VALUE
ASSETS:	
Cash in Savings Accounts	200
Cash in Checking Accounts	400
Certificates of Deposit (CDs)	
Cash on Hand	100
Money Market Accounts	
Money Owed to Me	
Cash Value of Life Insurance	2500
Savings Bonds (current value)	
Stocks (FB)	
Bonds	
Mutual Funds	
Vested Value of Stock Options	
Other Investments (Precious Metals)	
Individual Retirement Accounts	50000
Keogh Accounts	
401(k) or 403(b) Accounts	
Other Retirement Plans	
Market Value of Your Home	125000
Market Value of Other Real Estate	
Blue Book Value of Cars/Trucks	5000
Boats, Planes, Other Vehicles	
Jewelry	
Collectibles	
Furnishings	
Other	
TOTAL ASSETS	183200
LIABILITIES:	
Mortgages	100000
Car Loans	4000
Credit Card (Dept Store)	
Line of Credit	
Credit Card (Bank)	7000
Other Loans	
Credit Card	
School Loans	25000
Income Taxes Owed	
Other Taxes Owed	
Other Debts	
TOTAL LIABILITIES	136000
non-mortgage debt	136000
NET WORTH (TOTAL ASSETS LESS TOTAL LIABILITIES)	**47200**

Q&A (Questions & Actions)

What is your current net worth? (Assets minus liabilities)

Are you living paycheck to paycheck?

Have you recently bounced a check?

Have you ever had more month left than money to afford it?

Are all your important documents in a central location?

Choose a budgeting tool and start entering income and expenses this week.

Cut unneeded or excessive expenses.

Complete a net worth chart.

PHASE 4-PROTECT

From six calamities he will rescue you;
in seven no harm will touch you.
Job 5:19

Problem: One catastrophic event can totally wipe out your financial wellbeing. Sadly, far too many people are laden with debt and have little to no insurance coverage to protect them from catastrophes.

Solution: Obtain the proper amount of insurance and eliminate debt from your life. (and other measures to protect financial assets)

PHASE 4- PROTECT

April 7th, 2005 was one of the worst days of my life. It was the day my father died. He was my lifelong teacher, adviser, mentor, supporter, and friend. Years before his death, I had moved him and my mother back to my hometown from their retirement home in the south. His health was failing, and my mother was affected by dementia. It was good having my parents close by in their elderly years. We got them situated with an apartment and arranged to meet an attorney with them to get their affairs in order. We spent thousands on preparing their estate documents. I now have access to low-cost legal services that would have significantly reduced the overall cost. But nevertheless, the added stress of not knowing what to do or how to pay for my dad's final expenses was eliminated through wise and careful estate planning preparations and setting a burial fund aside in lieu of an insurance policy. As his power of attorney and later his executor, I was able to find a small insurance policy from his union affiliation. The average family without a life insurance policy or saved burial expenses has an increased level of stress and anxiety due to lack of estate planning. Protect yourself and your loved ones from unnecessary stress and financial hardship by obtaining the proper insurance and completing the proper estate documents now.

Understanding Insurance and Its Importance

Insurance is a financial product that is used to indemnify or protect us from unforeseen risk, loss, or financial burden by financially reimbursing us for that loss.

People who lack the financial recourses or insurance to recover from a loss or pay financial obligations are considered bankrupt.

People who have enough money to replace losses or monetary obligations without using insurance are considered self-insured.

NEVER, NEVER, NEVER cancel an insurance policy until you have a replacement policy "in hand."

The Most Common Types of Insurance

LIFE INSURANCE

Term vs. Whole Life (Buy term insurance and invest the difference in a stock market product like mutual funds.)

$500,000 Death Benefit

	30 Year Term	Whole Life
30 Years Old	$390	$5,376
40 Years Old	$618	$8,006
50 Years Old	$1,555	$12,726
	20 Year Term	**Whole Life**
60 Years Old	$2,417	$20,726
	15 Year Term	**Whole Life**
70 Years Old	$5,260	$35,166

Life insurance protects our heir's livelihood. It replaces the income of a loved one who was depended upon now that he or she is deceased.

Example: Insured/husband dies who brought home $75,000 after taxes. (Term) Insurance should be 10-12 times the take-home income, or $750,000 (face value).

Beneficiary/wife invests principal of $750,000 and lives off 10% interest, or $75,000.

HEALTH INSURANCE

Health insurance protects our savings from being dwindled away by high medical bills.

You pay a regular premium through your employer or directly to an insurance company. You then pay a little money at time of service (co-pay). Insurance pays the remaining medical cost, minus any yearly deductible amount.

HOMEOWNERS/RENTER'S INSURANCE

Homeowners or renter's insurance protects you from loss (theft, house damage, or lawsuit) associated to your residence. This is typically paid through your mortgage company if you have a mortgage.

There is generally a deductible, which means you pay a certain amount, and the insurance pays everything above that. The higher your deductible, the lower your monthly premium.

Example: You experience a storm that creates a hole in your roof, which leaks water into your property.

Try to use an insurance or claims adjuster because they work for you and only get paid when you do. Insurance companies typically want to pay as little as possible.

Your deductible is $1,000. The cost to repair is $5,000.

You then submit a claim and receive a check in the amount of $4,000.

AUTO INSURANCE

Auto insurance protects you against damages associated with your car.

Basic coverages:

- Liability covers you when you are at fault.

- Medical covers injuries of you or your passengers.

- Uninsured/Underinsured Motorist covers you when the other person lacks insurance.

- Vehicle Coverages covers damages to your car,

i.e. comprehensive, collision, towing, etc.

LONG-TERM DISABILITY INSURANCE

Long-term disability insurance protects our savings if we are unable to work for an extended period by providing a monthly income to help with expenses. Short-term disability should be taken care of with your emergency fund.

Long-term disabilities can last for months or even years, so the financial impact can be devastating. A disability that lasts for an extended period without a source of income can lead to car repossessions, mortgage foreclosures, and even personal bankruptcy. Unless your income will keep coming even if you can't go to work (i.e. residual income), you need to consider long-term disability insurance.

LONG-TERM CARE INSURANCE

This protects a person's retirement savings who has a chronic medical condition, disorder, or disability by covering the cost of homecare, assisted living, adult daycare, or nursing home cost.

Nursing home costs vary from state to state but can be around $200-$300 per day, which equals around $70,000-$110,000 per year. Without outside help or a sizable retirement fund, yours or your elderly loved one's funds will reduce rapidly. Then you or your loved one will be at the mercy of the government for help. Consider this insurance as you are approaching retirement and especially if you have little saved in your retirement fund.

Access to LEGAL SERVICES.

Access to legal services is very important, but most legal costs are higher than what the average person can afford. Lawyer's fees can drain your savings, but I have partnered in business with a company called Legal Shield, who gives you access to legal services for a low monthly fee, which is currently less than $1 a day. I am also in a position to market these services to others. One of the many services that they provide at no extra cost is will preparation. The average will can begin at $300 and up. The same documents I spent thousands on more than fifteen years ago for my mother and father, today I got for less than $1 a day.

If you are interested in learning more about low-cost legal services for you or your business, then check out my website: https://jbrown1x3.wearelegalshield.com (At the top right of the webpage, be sure to pick your home state, as plans vary from state to state.) Check out the other plans available and pick a plan today to enhance your financial wellness journey.

IDENTITY THEFT PROTECTION

This service protects you from identity theft. Criminals today can not only steal your money but also your identity. Legal Shield through its service ID Shield also provides access to identity theft protection for a low monthly fee.

If you are interested in learning more about identity theft protection, then check out my website:

https://jbrown1x3.wearelegalshield.com

(At the top right of the webpage, be sure to pick your home state, as plans vary from state to state.) Check out the other plans available and pick a plan today to enhance your financial wellness journey.

Use Other Protective Measures

Insurance alone will not cover every financial hardship or expense that we will face. How do you address the replacement of worn-down tires on your vehicle or the unexpected tax bill or a myriad of other unexpected expenses that can come your way? If you are like many people, you use debt, mostly in the form of credit cards, to handle the expenses insurance or cash will not resolve. Even our government uses debt to resolve financial shortages, so many people follow suit and incur debt as well. The problem is that the expense does not disappear but is just transferred to a company that is not only willing to help you with hardships but to finance your lifestyle as well. First, it was tires or your tax bill. Next thing you know, it is a new suit, car, or addition to your home. Who needs money when you can just charge it?

I understand the lure of debt because I have been there before. I battled my way back from bankruptcy and became very responsible with money. I handled the little debt I had so well that my credit score soared to over 700. Creditors were lining up at my door to give me credit. Like a fish in water, I took the bait. I applied for the gold card. I reasoned in my mind that I would pay off the balance every month and avoid interest charges. For months, I followed this plan to a tee, and then I got a letter congratulating me for being such a fine customer that they were offering me their extended payment option. I still kept my balance low, but the ability to extend payments gave me a sense of false security because, in reality, I was accumulating interest for them. One day, I called the customer service and asked what my credit limit was. To my amazement and surprise, the customer service rep told me that I did not have one. This news just happened to come when I was in the market for a new car. I resisted the temptation to charge a new car but reasoned within myself that if I bought a pre-owned car and kept the payment low, it would be a responsible thing to do. I eventually sold the car and used the proceeds to fund a bathroom remodel. This cycle of using debt to finance my lifestyle would likely have continued for the rest of my life, but I reached a point where I hated owing some creditor a large portion of my paycheck month after month, year after year. I decided I wanted to put debt permanently in my past and experience the freedom of knowing that none of my money was obligated to anyone when I got paid. Until you reach that point, you will always be in someone's debt.

**The poor are ruled by the rich,
and those who borrow are slaves of moneylenders.
Proverbs 22:7 (CEV)**

Whatever money we have that is not dwindled by loss can be dwindled by unwise spending, debt being among the most damaging to our financial wellbeing.

Good Debt vs. Bad Debt Is a Fallacy

There is only bad debt and even worse debt.

If a borrower is slave to the lender, then borrowers should be making every effort to free themselves from the bondage of the lender. You should not want to be a lifetime borrower any more than you would want to be a lifetime slave. All debt puts you at the mercy of moneylenders.

Worst of the Worst Debt Products

Payday Loans – Interest rates range from 390% to 780% APR.

Timeshare – Forced vacation fund, and they are almost impossible to get out of.

HELOC – Uses home equity to fund unsecured items.

Student Loans – Often, the loan amount is disproportionate to earning potential, and most can't be wiped out in bankruptcy.

Co-signed Loan – Basically, you agree to pay the loan off if the primary person defaults.

Car Lease – Lifelong rental.

Reverse Mortgage – You gain temporary relief with huge interest and fees.

401k Loan – You rob yourself of future growth.

Credit Cards – Give a false sense of wealth.

The Truth about Credit Bureaus

The credit bureaus (Equifax, Experian, and TransUnion) are actually for-profit companies that have shareholders. For example, TransUnion is owned by Goldman Sachs.

Credit bureaus primarily sell four data products: credit services, decision analytics, marketing, and consumer assistance services.

Credit Services: i.e. Consumer credit reports, which the bureau sells to lenders.

Decision Analytics: They sell lenders detailed analytics about the way an individual interacts with certain debt.

Marketing: Pre-approved credit lenders pay a marketing fee to a credit bureau.

Consumer Services: i.e. Credit monitoring, due to the increased threat of identity theft.

> **"Flat out, I believe the campaign for healthy credit is a marketing strategy perpetuated by the credit bureaus and banks. Healthy credit is the false aim, yet debt is the result."**
> **-petetheplanner.com**

FICO SCORE BREAKDOWN

A MEASUREMENT OF DEBT
10% NEW CREDIT
15% LENGTH OF CREDIT HISTORY
10% CREDIT MIX
35% PAYMENT HISTORY
30% AMOUNTS OWED
100% BASED ON DEBT

[5] Free yourself, like a gazelle from the hand of the hunter,
like a bird from the snare of the fowler.
Proverbs 6:5 (NIV)

Steps to Getting Out of Debt

Stop incurring new debt.

Stop using credit cards and cut them up.

List debt from small to largest (ignore the interest rates).

Pay all debt minimum payments and apply budget surplus to smallest debt until that debt is payed off (close credit account).

Apply same amount plus previous payment to next debt and repeat the process until all debts are gone.

Ideally, this process should take two years or less. If not, you need to increase income or sell some items to shorten the debt payment period.

Keep applying the same amount to create a savings account that equals 3-6 months' worth of expenses.

DEBT REDUCTION PLAN

DEBT REDUCTION EXCELARATOR	OUTSTAND BALANCE	START					END	MONTHS LEFT
Car Loans -SOLD	0	0	0	0	0	0	0	0
School Loans	7500	105	105	105	105	549	(105+444=271)	13
Department Store	5,100	75	75	75	444	(75+369=444)		11
Personal Loan	3400	65	65	369	(65+304=369)			9
Credit Card #2	750	33	304	(33+271=304)				2
Credit Card #1	375	271	(26+245=271)					2
	17125	549	549	549	549	549	0	37

Q&A (Question & Actions)

Are debt collectors bothering you regularly?

Can you handle a $500 emergency without borrowing?

Do you have an up-to-date will?

Would your dependents be fine financially if you were to die?

Cut up all your credits cards today.

Close each credit account once card is paid off.

Contact an insurance broker this week or get several insurance quotes on your own.

PHASE 5- SAVE

A good person leaves an inheritance
for their children's children,
Proverbs 13:22a

Problem: Many people save far too little of their income to benefit the next generation because their wealth is committed to debtors and not their heirs.

Solution: Saving should be a regular and significant item in your budget. Use an emergency fund to help you deal with unexpected expenses and save money toward wealth building and other major purchases.

PHASE 5- SAVE

As I stated earlier, my father taught me the value of saving from an early age, but what I discovered in my late teens would take my saving mindset to another level. I learned how multi-generational wealth is created through the stock market. My father kept away from the stock market because he didn't understand it, but it has long been a secret enjoyed by the rich and hidden from the average person. Now anyone with a smart-phone can download an app and be investing within minutes. Banks have traditionally given away only single-digit interest to customers while charging double-digit interest for loans and other products. No one will ever get rich by earning single-digit interest while at the same time paying double-digit interest. You should have a portion of your money saved/invested in the stock market.

Saving vs. Investing

Investing is a logical progression from saving. It is just saving with higher returns and risk, but the rewards of investing have proven over history that it is worth the risk. Nevertheless, saving and having at least 3-6 months of emergency funds set aside should be accomplished before investing. Investing is a long-term process, and the uncertainties of life can happen in the interim. Having an emergency fund will allow it to grow without unnecessary withdrawals that a savings/emergency account should be able to handle.

What Is the Stock Market?

The stock market is an actual and virtual place where you can buy and sell portions of companies. This happens at a place called a stock exchange. The New York Stock Exchange is among the most famous and largest. Stocks give you an ownership portion or share of a publicly-traded company. Private companies can't provide shares to the general public, only to employees and board members. A person who owns shares in a company is called a shareholder. Investing in stocks literally gives you the ability to own a portion of a company. The financial service industry has organized these stocks into financial products you can buy and sell. The stock exchange tracks the price of each share, which goes up and down based primarily on the performance of the company. Other factors can affect the price like wars, pandemics, politics, etc. You can buy individual shares of one company or buy a product that already has the stocks grouped together. I do not recommend beginners buy individual stocks. There is standard grouping called indexes or more customized grouping put together by brokerage companies within the financial service industry. Some of the standard grouping include the S&P 500, which is a grouping of the 500 largest companies in America, the Dow Jones, which is the 30 largest companies in America, and the NASDAQ, which has thousands of companies. Most other groupings of stocks are measured on their ability to outperform these three indexes. Other groupings can be based on the size of companies' earnings (i.e. large, medium, small) or the industry (e.g. healthcare, energy, real estate). Traditionally, the primary financial product used to invest in multiple companies was mutual funds. Mutual funds grouped many companies together to provide diversification, which lowered your risk from the loss of just one company failing. You now have the ability to invest directly into the index funds, which bypasses many of the fees traditionally charged by mutual fund companies. You can purchase mutual funds or other financial products online, directly from a brokerage firm (e.g. Vanguard, Charles Schwab, Fidelity, TD Ameritrade, etc.), through your employer, or from a certified financial adviser. Before actually investing, I recommend you talk with a fiduciary. A fiduciary is a financial advisor who is fee-based and not commission-based. In other words, they have a primary financial obligation to you and not to the companies that pay high commissions to sell their products.

How Should You Proceed?

The sequence of your steps when managing your money will either speed up and slow down your progress. It is more important sometimes to concentrate on one task at a time and finish it within a reasonable time period then to try to do everything at the same time and never finish anything.

Setting up an emergency fund of $1,000-2,000 immediately is a priority because this will give you a cushion for short-term emergencies and help you resist going into more debt.

Once you have a small emergency fund, then you should focus on paying off all consumer debt (i.e. student loans, credit cards, car loans, tax bills).

After you've paid off all consumer debt, you can then start saving 3-6 months' worth of monthly expenses in a full emergency fund.

You now are prepared to begin real wealth building by setting aside and investing 15% of your gross income.

Do's and Don'ts of Investing

Do invest early. The sooner you start, the more your money can grow.

Do invest regularly and consistently. Set aside the same amount weekly or monthly. This is sometimes referred to as dollar cost averaging. When stocks are low, you buy more, and when they're high, you buy less. This method has been proven to be more profitable than trying to time the market and buy stock at special times.

Do leave your money in for the long term. The price of stocks goes up and down, but history has proven that it has trended upward.

Do make saving/investing an automatic event. Have it debited from your bank or paycheck automatically. The less you see it, the easier it is to save.

Don't invest before having your 3-6-month emergency fund. There are risks associated with the stock market, and you should not invest money you may need for emergencies.

Don't borrow or make early withdrawals from your investment funds unless it is for extreme emergencies (e.g. bankruptcy, foreclosure, major illness, etc.).

Don't withdraw all your money out of fear when the price drops. Prices rise and fall all the time, but they have always trended upward over the long run.

Primary Reasons to Save

Emergencies, wealth building, and major purchases

Emergencies

This money will typically be in a very safe, low-risk place where you can get to it quickly. For example: savings account, money market account, home safe, shoebox, etc. Don't worry about the interest rate because this is savings, not a real investment. You will likely need it within the next six months to a year. Replenish it as you use it. It should always be maintained at least at the 3-6-month level.

Wealth Building

This money will have to be placed in a brokerage account that has some increased risk but has historically increased exponentially. These investments are typically kept for at least three years or more with the goal of using them for retirement. Interest rate is more important here because we want the money to grow. We reduce our risk by diversifying or spreading our investing over multiple companies using indexes or mutual funds.

For example:

Yearly income is $25,000/invest $3,750 yearly/$313 monthly

Yearly income is $50,000/invest $7,500 yearly/$625 monthly

Yearly income is $100,000/invest $15,000 yearly/$1,250 monthly

A little bit grows to be a lot:

15% a year for a person making $16,000 yearly

Only $200/month for 40 years @12%

Date	Contribution	Interest	Balance
Year One	$0.00	$0.00	$200.00
Year 2	$2,400.00	$312.00	$2,912.00
Year 3	$2,400.00	$637.44	$5,949.44
Year 4	$2,400.00	$1,001.93	$9,351.37
Year 5	$2,400.00	$1,410.16	$13,161.53
Year 10	$2,400.00	$5,120.59	$47,792.16
Year 20	$2,400.00	$20,957.81	$195,606.22
Year 30	$2,400.00	$70,145.81	$654,694.26
Year 40	$2,400.00	$222,916.28	$2,080,551.97

Common IRS Treatment of Investment Accounts.

401(k) For Profit Companies/403(b) or TSA (Tax-sheltered Annuity) Non-Profit Companies– Purchased pre-tax through employer, usually has a percentage match with a max amount yearly

Roth IRA (Individual Retirement Account) – taxed up front but grows tax free.

Regularly consult with your attorney, financial advisor, and accountant about how to lawfully minimize taxes to maximize wealth building.

Major Purchases

After you have paid off all consumer debt, saved 3-6 months' worth of monthly expenses, set aside 15% of your gross income for investing, and put away money for your kids' college education, then start saving for major purchases. Some of these major purchases include: your house, car, and vacations.

I talk more about house buying in the next chapter, but you should establish separate funds beyond your emergency and investments to handle larger purchases that can't be handled in your monthly budget. For example: If you can finance a car by paying $400 every month for 4-5 years, then you can buy a low-cost car for cash and save the same $400 per month in a car purchase fund.

"It's not how much money you make, but how much money you keep, how hard it works for you, and how many generations you keep it for."
-Robert Kiyosaki

Q&A (Question & Actions)

How long could you live off what you currently have saved?

How many generations will your money last?

How much money do you need monthly to live well in retirement?

Where would you go or what would you do if money was no longer a factor?

The best time to invest is right now. Make an appointment with a fiduciary and begin a conversation about wealth building.

Have a garage sale, get another source of income, and cut expenses to grow an emergency fund fast.

Halt your current retirement payroll deductions to help grow your emergency fund faster.

PHASE 6- SPEND

[15] Then he said to them, "Watch out! Be on your guard against all kinds of greed; life does not consist in an abundance of possessions."
Luke 12:15 (NIV)

Problem: We have not resisted inward and outward pressure to accumulate stuff that we neither use nor needed in the first place.

Solution: Prioritize your spending and learn to say no to spending that does not align with your budget and goals. Give, Save, and then Spend.

"Too many people spend money they haven't earned to buy things they don't want to impress people they don't like."
Will Rogers

PHASE 6- SPEND

You do not have to spend a lot to get a lot. I once bought a car for only $325. My father and I went to a local car auction. Like many auctions, the fancy and pristine items get all the attention and spark a bidding war. But many items are overlooked entirely, and those are the diamonds in the rough. We arrived early, signed in, and began to scan the large inventory of vehicles. We knew what our budget was and spotted several cars that fell within our limit. Then the car that would become mine came up on the auction block. It was a grey station wagon with some front bumper damage. The auctioneer started with, "We are going to start the bidding with $325." I raised my paddle, and within a minute, he shouted, "Sold for $325." I was the only person who bid, and it was all mine. After paying for the car, I began the next phase of ownership. We had the car towed home and waited for the state to send my papers before I could drive it. In the meantime, I had a locksmith make keys for it. The car was likely the product of repossession or impounding that the person never reclaimed. Nevertheless, by the time I was able to drive the car, I had only spent about $600 total. I drove that car nearly a year with no repairs or mechanical-related costs. I now own two cars with no payments, and it feels good!

Change Your Budget, Change Your Life

The budget below is the same budget presented in the Phase 3-TRACK chapter. This budget represents some changes I would recommend to someone I was counseling. The first column is the current budget, and the second column is the revised budget. This example shows how you can make very small adjustments to improve your spending while freeing up a surplus every month. The $271 that was freed up at the bottom of the budget could be applied to debt repayment, then to an emergency fund, and lastly to investments.

MONTH (PLAN EACH MONTH/ NO YEARLY BUDGET)		
INCOME	PROJECTED (INITIAL)	PROJECTED (CORRECTED)
PRIMARY INCOME (T4) wow)	3000	3000
OVERTIME	200	500
PART-TIME	50	100
Other 1		
Other 2		
TOTAL (INCOME AND EXPENCES SHOULD MATCH)	3250	3600
EXPENCES	**PROJECTED (INITIAL)**	**PROJECTED (CORRECTED)**
GIVING (10%-15%)		
TITHES	50	300
OFFERINGS	10	10
OTHER	5	50
SAVING (10%-15%)		
EMERGENCY FUND	0	300
RETIREMENT (15%)	0	0
HOUSING (25%-35%)		
MORTGAGE/RENT	1000	1000
ELECTRIC	150	150
GAS	150	150
WATER AND SEWER	50	50
CABLE	200	0
PHONE		40
CELL PHONE	125	45
INTERNET	0	40
OTHER		
TRANSPORTATION		
CAR PAYMENT (LIST IN DEBT)		
BUS FARE	96	96
GASOLINE	60	0
CAR WASH		
MAINTINENCE		
OTHER		
FOOD		
GROCERIES	215	275
DINING OUT	185	50
OTHER		
LIFESTYLE		
CLOTHING	100	25
HAIR	120	60
DRY CLEANING	75	25
GYM MEMBERSHIP	35	10
DAYCARE	600	325
TUITION		
PETS		
GIFT		
OTHER	50	50
OTHER		
INSURANCE		
HOME/RENTERS		
AUTO	200	0
LIFE		
HEALTH		
DISABILITY		
LONG-TERM CARE		
OTHER		
DEBT		
CAR NOTE	400	0
STUDENT LOAN	105	105
DEPARTMENT STORE	75	75
PERSONAL LOAN	65	65
CREDIT CARD	33	33
CREDIT CARD	26	271
OTHER		
OTHER		
TOTAL	4180	3600
DIFFERENCE	-930	0

Our Spending Should Also Be Goal-Driven

Goals drive you, motivate you, and empower you.

Make daily, weekly, monthly, yearly, and lifetime goals.

**"If you aim at nothing, you'll hit it every time."
Zig Ziglar**

Goals affect how you spend money. If you have a goal to be debt-free, then every purchase you make will help or harm your goal.

Example: "I will completely eliminate all my consumer debt of $6,500 by May of 2023" vs "One day, I'm going to get out of debt."

Goals should be:

Specific – All consumer debt ($$$ amount), not home

Measurable – The amount and end date stated.

Attainable – You have a $271 monthly surplus (see budget above)

Realistic – It did not say debt-free by next month!

Time sensitive – May of 2023

Learn How to Spend Wisely

Think frugally or thriftily versus extravagantly—not cheap, not wasteful, not regularly making unnecessary purchases but being a careful spender. Negotiate when possible. Ask yourself questions. Beware of entitlement thinking: "I deserve it."

Seek wise counsel.

Check your budget.

Think needs vs wants vs desires.

Duplicate the spending habits of rich people.

The average millionaire does not look rich.

They drive modest used cars and pay cash.

Shop at bargain stores, clip coupons, buy staple items in bulk, and consider pre-owned items when possible.

Rich people don't spend wisely when they become rich; they become rich because they spend wisely.

Understand and Resist External Influences on Your Spending

Let's consider some ads to learn advertising tricks and schemes.

Cosmetic giant L'Oreal introduced an ad that simply read, "Because you're worth it." Women believe the message and spend hundreds or even thousands a year on cosmetics without even considering the high prices.

Why are diamonds associated with weddings? Because the diamond industry has cleverly marketed the diamond as the must-have for engagements and weddings. Consequently, a young couple will spend more on their rings than they will on a down payment to their new home.

NIKE has a slogan that most people identify with, "Just Do It." Just do what? Should I spend $250 on a pair of sneakers and have $0 invested in the company?

Does drinking soda make you this happy? Many soft drink ads have happy smiling people, but there are no smiles when your dentist tells you that you have several cavities or your doctor tells you that you have diabetes.

Ads create brand recognition. There are many products that we associate the name in exchange for the generic item's name:

e.g. Band–Aid vs. adhesive bandage, Xerox vs. copier, Kleenex vs. tissue, etc. Always shop around before just agreeing to buy the name brand items.

Famous Person Appeal

He has one, so I want to be like him.

Many ads feature famous people we love and admire. We concentrate on the person and ignore the price. The item is likely a small percentage of his or her net worth compared to the average person.

> **"If advertisers spent the same amount of money on improving their products as they do on advertising then they wouldn't have to advertise them."**
> **-Will Rogers**

Your Largest Purchase

Small purchases drain your finances slowly, but the wrong large purchase can set you back financially for years. Real estate still remains one of the largest purchases you will make in your lifetime.

Guidelines for Buying A House

Purpose to get out of consumer debt before buying a house. Purpose to stay out of debt.

Also have a 3-6-month emergency savings fund in place.

Save to have a 10% or more down payment. That way you have equity in the property from the first day.

Your monthly mortgage payment (including tax and insurance) should not exceed 25% of your take-home pay.

Always know what other like properties in the area are on sale for, have sold for, and are listed as. You can do this by asking your realtor for a comparative market analysis.

EXAMPLE: Let's say, you want to buy a property for $200,000, but other like properties in the area are being sold for $175,000. Should you buy? This is not an ideal situation.

On the other hand, you want to buy a property for $175,000, but other like properties in the area are being sold for $200,000. Should you buy? This situation is more ideal.

Some buys are like diamonds in the rough. If you don't have an eye to spot needed repairs, then use a home inspector with a contingency clause that basically says that you can walk away from the agreement if repairs exceed a certain dollar amount.

That's why savings are important because you might have to make some minor repairs to get the best deal on a property.

The three most popular words in real estate are:

LOCATION, LOCATION, LOCATION!

Location matters, so look at neighborhood trends, visit the location at various times of the day, and talk to current residents.

Buying a House

Renting can be a good short-term solution. Most mortgage payments in the first few years are primarily interest payments.

SIMPLE LOAN CALCULATOR

LOAN VALUES	
Loan amount	$200,000.00
Annual interest rate	4.13%
Loan period in years	15
Start date of loan	5/1/2019

LOAN SUMMARY	
Monthly payment	$1,491.94
Number of payments	180
Total interest	$68,548.33
Total cost of loan	$268,548.33

PMT NO.	PAYMENT DATE	BEGINNING BALANCE	PAYMENT	PRINCIPAL	INTEREST	ENDING BALANCE
1	6/1/2019	$200,000.00	$1,491.94	$804.44	$687.50	$199,195.56
2	7/1/2019	$199,195.56	$1,491.94	$807.20	$684.73	$198,388.36
3	8/1/2019	$198,388.36	$1,491.94	$809.98	$681.96	$197,578.39
4	9/1/2019	$197,578.39	$1,491.94	$812.76	$679.18	$196,765.63
5	10/1/2019	$196,765.63	$1,491.94	$815.55	$676.38	$195,950.08
6	11/1/2019	$195,950.08	$1,491.94	$818.36	$673.58	$195,131.72
7	12/1/2019	$195,131.72	$1,491.94	$821.17	$670.77	$194,310.55
8	1/1/2020	$194,310.55	$1,491.94	$823.99	$667.94	$193,486.56
9	2/1/2020	$193,486.56	$1,491.94	$826.83	$665.11	$192,659.73
10	3/1/2020	$192,659.73	$1,491.94	$829.67	$662.27	$191,830.06

Owning a home is a better long-term solution to wealth building.

As you make payments on your mortgage, the last few payments will be primarily principal payments.

SIMPLE LOAN CALCULATOR

LOAN VALUES

Loan amount	$200,000.00
Annual interest rate	4.13%
Loan period in years	15
Start date of loan	5/1/2019

LOAN SUMMARY

Monthly payment	$1,491.94
Number of payments	180
Total interest	$68,548.33
Total cost of loan	$268,548.33

PMT NO.	PAYMENT DATE	BEGINNING BALANCE	PAYMENT	PRINCIPAL	INTEREST	ENDING BALANCE
169	6/1/2033	$17,509.53	$1,491.94	$1,431.75	$60.19	$16,077.79
170	7/1/2033	$16,077.79	$1,491.94	$1,436.67	$55.27	$14,641.12
171	8/1/2033	$14,641.12	$1,491.94	$1,441.61	$50.33	$13,199.51
172	9/1/2033	$13,199.51	$1,491.94	$1,446.56	$45.37	$11,752.95
173	10/1/2033	$11,752.95	$1,491.94	$1,451.53	$40.40	$10,301.42
174	11/1/2033	$10,301.42	$1,491.94	$1,456.52	$35.41	$8,844.89
175	12/1/2033	$8,844.89	$1,491.94	$1,461.53	$30.40	$7,383.36
176	1/1/2034	$7,383.36	$1,491.94	$1,466.55	$25.38	$5,916.81
177	2/1/2034	$5,916.81	$1,491.94	$1,471.60	$20.34	$4,445.21
178	3/1/2034	$4,445.21	$1,491.94	$1,476.65	$15.28	$2,968.55
179	4/1/2034	$2,968.55	$1,491.94	$1,481.73	$10.20	$1,486.82
180	5/1/2034	$1,486.82	$1,491.94	$1,486.82	$5.11	$0.00

Buying a House

A 15-year mortgage is a far better option than a 30-year mortgage.

Simple Loan Calculator

	Enter values
Loan amount	$ 150,000.00
Annual interest rate	3.09%
Loan period in years	15
Start date of loan	7/1/2017

Monthly payment	$ 1,042.38
Number of payments	180
Total interest	$ 37,627.96
Total cost of loan	$ 187,627.96

Simple Loan Calculator

	Enter values
Loan amount	$ 150,000.00
Annual interest rate	3.88%
Loan period in years	30
Start date of loan	7/1/2017

Monthly payment	$ 705.78
Number of payments	360
Total interest	$ 104,082.49
Total cost of loan	$ 254,082.49

Buying a House

After 15 years is paid, you can invest the prior mortgage payment of $1,042.38 over the next 15 years @ 12% and make... (see below)

Invest	Old mortgage payment of $1,042.38
Over Next 15 years	@ 12% Interest Rate of return
You Contribute	$187,560
It grow with interest to	$526,810

"Do's and Don'ts" of Buying a House

Do your research.

Do get pre-approved for a mortgage.

Do have someone representing you in the transaction (buying broker or lawyer).

Do screen the person representing you.

Do read the contract carefully.

Do buy title insurance.

Do set up bi-weekly payments on your mortgage.

Do ask questions.

Don't be in a rush.

Don't buy more than you can afford.

Don't use horrible mortgage options.

Don't buy on emotions.

Don't buy the first property you see.

Don't be afraid to negotiate.

Don't try to be like the Joneses.

"Never spend your money before you have earned it."
Thomas Jefferson

Q&A (Questions & Actions)

Do you have a problem saying no to sales pitches?

What advice would you give to yourself 5, 10, 20, 30 years ago?

What do you want to achieve 1 year from now? ... 3 years? ... 5 years? ... 10 years?

Go through your home and give away or sell unneeded or unused items.

Use cash when shopping to avoid overspending.

Stop comparing yourself to others and appreciate what you have.

PHASE 7- ENJOY

[13] And people should eat and drink and enjoy the fruits of
their labor, for these are gifts from God.
Ecclesiastes 3:13 (NLT)

Problem: Most people have a microwave view of enjoyment
rather than a slow-cooker view of enjoyment. Improper financial planning leads to a cycle of enjoyment followed by regret.

Solution: Proper financial planning leaves a person debt
free and wealthy so he or she can experience enjoyment
without regret.

PHASE 7 - ENJOY

No matter how much money you earn, you can find a way to enjoy it. In fact, some forms of enjoyment are free. A simple walk in the park or calling your best friend are great cost-free ways to enjoy life. But since this book is about money, how can you spend your money in a way that brings joy? My wife and I made a commitment to go on vacation at least once every year. When we began to have children, the need or commitment to take a yearly vacation was even greater. We wanted to build memories that would last a lifetime. The vacations varied from a short stay in a local hotel to visiting extended family to a long stay at popular sites like Walt Disney World. We also made a commitment to save money or use a tax return to build a vacation fund and avoid going into debt.

I hear stories about people who have worked forty years and only missed several days or the person who brags that he or she only took one vacation in ten years. On the surface, it sounds like a very strong work ethic, but beneath the surface, I believe these people missed the great opportunity to enjoy life and build lasting memories. It actually helps you to do your job better when you take time off to replenish your strength and rejuvenate your mind. If traveling is not the thing that gives you joy, discover what does and commit to using your hard-earned money for more than just paying bills.

Enjoy Within Your Means

Do not be tempted to duplicate the fun times that sometimes can be displayed on social media. Many times, the picture does not tell the full or true story. Forget about the Joneses; they're miserable, broke, and one paycheck away from being homeless.

Enjoy your life and not theirs. Stop the comparison game.

Be content. Grow where you are planted.

What does this number

represent?

The number 29,200 represents the amount of days in the average person's life. If a person lives to be 80 years old, he or she would have lived 29,200 days. If we really break that number down...

If we sleep an average of 8 hours per night, we would have slept 26.6 of our 80 years, or a third of our lives.

Invest in a good mattress without going into debt. Treat yourself to high thread-count sheets that feel like silk. Buy a comfortable pillow. These are several ways you can enjoy the time you sleep and wake up feeling well-rested and rejuvenated.

If we work an average of 40 hours per week for 30 years, we would have actually worked 21.5 of our 80 years. Aim to make your work a place that is fun and fulfilling.

If we eat an average of 2 hours per day for 80 years, we would have actually spent time eating 6.6 of our 80 years.

I share all these numbers with you to emphasize the fact that life is short no matter how long we live. So, live it without regret.

Enjoyment Suggestions

Buy art or visit an art museum regularly.

Start a collection of items that make you smile.

Have a regular date night with your spouse or significant other at least once a week.

Declutter your home environment.

Create a bucket list and start completing it.

A Happy Life

In addition to financial freedom, peace of mind, and meaningful relationships; being healthy is one of the top things to help you enjoy life.

Your Health Matters -Steps to Maintaining a Healthy Lifestyle

Eat Right – All things in moderation. Balanced meals. If God makes it, it's good; if man makes it, beware.

Exercise – three to four times per week – combination of stretching, cardio, strength training.

Stay away from harmful substances – smoking, drinking, drugs, etc.

Get the proper amount of sleep

Regular doctor's visits–Check-up, dentist, eye doctor, other specialist, etc.

"Take care of your body. It's the only place you have to live."
-Jim Rohn

Everybody – A Poem by Joe Brown

Everybody has a voice, so use it to speak.

Everybody wants more time, so make the best of your week.

Everybody wants conversation, so start to talk.

Everybody wants to lose weight, so start to walk.

Everybody wants money, so you have to save.

Everybody wants things, but don't be a slave.

Everybody wants love, but don't look in the wrong places.

Everybody wants joy, so what's with the long faces?

Everybody wants knowledge, so you have to read.

Everybody wants help, but don't live by greed.

Everybody takes, but not everyone gives.

Everybody dies, but not everyone lives.

Everybody has resources, so don't abuse it.

Everybody has time; be careful how you use it.

Everybody wants to be built up, so don't destroy.

Everybody wants to be happy, so choose to enjoy.

Everybody! Everybody! Everybody!

Q&A (Question & Actions)

Do you neglect any part of your health? (diet, fitness, rest, doctor's visits)

If you had an extra $20,000, how would you enjoy it?

Are people enabling you or holding you back?

Schedule a doctor's visit to check some aspect of your health.

Start an activity in your daily schedule that gives you joy.

Set aside an item in your budget specifically for enjoyment.

ACTION PLANS

Action Plan for Next 7 Days

(EARN)- Begin dreaming about ideal job.

(GIVE)-Identify a small way to give.

(TRACK)- Complete a preliminary budget

(PROTECT)-Identify insurances and debts.

(SAVE)- Start building $1,000 emergency fund.

(SPEND)-Stick to your budget. Needs first.

(ENJOY)-Congratulate yourself for taking action.

Action Plan for Next 7 Weeks

(EARN)- Create or find an additional income source.

(GIVE)-Set aside a giving amount in budget.

(TRACK)- Track all spending to match budget.

(PROTECT)-Verify insurance coverages and debts.

(SAVE)- Continue building $1,000 emergency fund.

(SPEND)-Stick to your budget. Needs first.

(ENJOY)-Treat yourself for moving in the right direction.

Action Plan for Next 7 Months

(EARN)- Dedicate time each week to grow your second income.

(GIVE)-Find regular ways to give of your time, talent, and treasure.

(TRACK)- Become an expert at living on a budget.

(PROTECT)-Shop around and get the proper amount of insurance and put extra money toward paying off smallest debt using "debt reduction accelerator."

(SAVE)- Finish building $1,000 emergency fund and put extra funds toward debt reduction.

(SPEND)-Stick to your budget. Needs first.

(ENJOY)-Have a low-cost celebration for moving in the right direction.

Action Plan for Next 7 Years and Beyond

(EARN)- Start working part-time or full-time in your dream job.

(GIVE)-Increase ways to give of your time, talent, and treasure.

(TRACK)- Consumer debt payments should be eliminated from your budget for the rest of your life. Keep living on a budget.

(PROTECT)-Reevaluate insurance needs and shop around for better prices. Pay off all consumer debt using "debt reduction accelerator."

(SAVE)- Finish building 3-6-month emergency fund.

(SPEND)-After emergency fund is complete, put 15% toward retirement and kids' education fund and start paying off mortgage.

(ENJOY)-Pay cash to complete at least one item on your bucket list and continue building wealth, giving, and enjoying life.

MOVE TO THE NEXT PHASE

Joe Brown

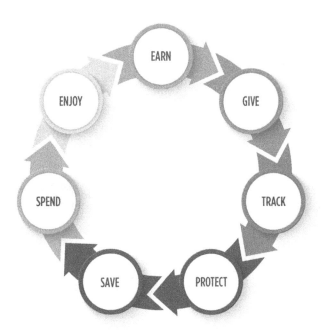

This is me in front of vault door of Federal Reserve Bank that was converted into a hotel.

CPSIA information can be obtained
at www.ICGtesting.com
Printed in the USA
LVHW081911050721
691893LV00014B/1193